the
Quick & Easy Guide
to IT Contracting
in the UK

Shane Sekuloski

Contents

About the Author

My credentials for writing this book are simply that I've "been there and done it" in the world of IT Contracting.

Originally from Sydney, Australia, I have been based in Central London since 2004 working on contracts predominantly in the Finance and Investment Banking industries for London-based clients with European operations. In total, I have been in the IT contracting business for 11 years.

My clients in London have included Barclays Bank, Citigroup, Brit Insurance, and JPMorgan Chase. My Australian clients have included Deloitte Touche Tohmatsu, IBM Global Services Australia, Westpac Bank, and AAP Communications Services.

My aim in this quick-and-easy guide is not to blow your mind with the myriad intricacies of the IT contracting world, but to tell you what you need to know (and no more) about making the move from permanent employment to contracting with clients. Think of it like you're picking the brains of your contractor mate down the pub.

Shane Sekuloski

the
Quick & Easy Guide
to **IT Contracting**
in the **UK**

1 – So you want to be an IT Contractor?

I know what you're thinking.

You're sitting at your 'permanent' desk in your 'permanent' job, and you glance enviously at the guy (or girl) sitting next to you. He (let's assume) is sitting at a desk that looks just as 'permanent' as yours, and he's been working at this company just as long as you have – about 18 months. He's doing exactly the same job as you, but as an independent contractor he's getting paid at least twice as much money to do it. He also gets to keep more of the money tax-free, but we'll come onto that. For the moment, let's look at how much nicer his car is than yours.

This apparent inequality – okay, let's call it "unfairness" – has been getting to you for some time, and it shows. No matter how many times you challenge this guy on the apparent unfairness, as if it's his fault, he has the ultimate comeback:

"If you think it's so great, why don't you do it?"

He's got a point. Why don't *you* do it? If you can't beat them, join them, so to speak.

As you start to think about it more deeply, you begin to get a little bit scared. Would you still get paid if you took ill for a week? Would you get any maternity or paternity leave and pay if you were blessed with a pregnancy? Could you cope with "doing your own tax" while operating as a limited company with a one-person PAYE scheme?

It's all starting to sound a little too much like hard work, and a little too uncertain for your tastes, so you continue as you have been. And you continue to seethe.

Let me tell you that making the transition from employee to independent contractor need not be as burdensome as you might think from an administrative perspective. If you don't fancy setting up your own limited company, you could always work through an agency as a pseudo-employee but (over time) for a range of end clients; or you could operate via an 'umbrella' company that will give you a PAYE salary plus a generous benefits package while you leave it to deal with Companies House and the HMRC. What I'm saying is that while your own limited company may be the *best* route, it's not the *only* route.

If you're still worried about the security of your employment, let me tell you that your one month notice period at your current employer may provide no more security than the one month notice period documented in your independent 'contract'. Sure, a permanent employee could benefit from a generous redundancy pay-out after a long term of service, and it's certainly worth hanging on in there if you think you might get one soon. But if not, you might consider looking at the 'security' of your employment from another perspective:

If you can secure a contract rate of twice your current salary – and it could be a lot more – then for every month you work on contract you will bank an extra month's income. On this basis: as soon as you have worked on contract for six months, you have bought yourself an additional six months 'security' to tide you over between jobs.

Do you really want to be secure in (or stuck with) your current employment when instead you can achieve the kind of personal security just described?

It doesn't stop there. You get added security from knowing that as a flexible mobile contractor who has obtained a range of cutting-edge skills in a number of client environments, you will always be able to find work somewhere in the UK or elsewhere in the world. How cool would it be to *get paid* for experiencing a foreign culture rather than paying for a holiday? And when I say 'foreign culture', I don't mean the short hop from London to Glasgow!

Having gone some way to convincing you that IT contracting is something of a no-brainer for many IT staff, I should of course mention that everything in the contracting garden is not rosy. There are some pitfalls and pratfalls for the unwary, and in the remainder of this "warts-n-all" guide I'll tell you what they are.

If you've already been made redundant, or you're otherwise out of work, you'll have very little to lose by trying to land your first contract. If you're in a dead-end but 'steady' job you'll be reluctant to hand in your notice until you've found a good first contract role. In either case, the first thing you need to think about is *Finding Contract Work*.

the
Quick & Easy Guide
to **IT Contracting**
in the **UK**

2 – Finding Contract Work

Before you can do any contract work, you of course need to find some contract work, and in this chapter we'll explore some of the many ways in which you can find the work.

Job Sites

The stalwart job site for IT contractors is the one at www.jobserve.com, which began in the 1990s as a job site primarily for IT staff and which has since expanded into advertising jobs for accountants, engineers and other professionals.

In the years BIE (Before the Internet Era) many IT staff would have looked for their next job in the back of the IT industry magazine Computer Weekly, which subsequently launched its own job site at www.cwjobs.co.uk. Despite a change of ownership – it's now run by Totaljobs Group – this web site still specialises in advertising jobs for IT professionals.

Another job site worth visiting is the Technojobs web site at www.technojobs.co.uk, and of course there are others, but any contracts you see listed on the less popular job sites are just as likely to be found on the main job sites listed above.

While there are other generic recruitment web sites such as the one at www.monster.com, it is probably true to say that IT contractors are best served by the historically IT-specific job sites just mentioned.

When you use one of these job sites, be sure to select the *Contract* option from the pull-down selection of *Contract* or *Permanent*, so that you don't inadvertently find yourself landing a brand new permanent employment! And if you don't want the overhead of checking through the listings every day, most job sites allow you to set up a facility for receiving suitable jobs advertisements (based on criteria you specify) by email.

On the Contractor UK web site at www.contractoruk.com you will even find a one-stop-shop IT Contract Search facility that pulls in jobs from the three main contractor job sites: CW Jobs, JobServe, and Technojobs.

Agencies

When you respond to one of the job advertisements on a job site, the chances are good that you will be referred to the agency that posted the job. It's mostly agencies rather than end clients who post the job advertisements.

Another option, therefore, is to browse the agencies' own web sites directly; or to register with those agencies by uploading you CV.

One problem with this approach is that in the IT world your CV can quickly become out-of-date so that it no longer reflects your current skills and interests. You could end up for the rest of your life receiving emails telling about the latest greatest Java job—even though you moved over to .NET programming in 2003!

Another problem with this approach is that not all employment and recruitment agencies have their own fully functional job sites, so many of them rely on JobServe (and others) for advertising their jobs.

If you do decide to register with an agency, you should register with several of them and not feel obliged to be 'loyal' to just one agency. Despite what their marketing materials and consultants' patter might lead you to believe, these agencies can be rather fickle... and therefore so can you be.

You will often see what looks suspiciously like *exactly the same job* advertised by more than one agency, and you might like to pursue the opportunity through the agency that seems to be offering the best rate; or the one that you trust the most.

Networking and Social Networking

As you get more and more contracts under your belt, and as you move from client to client, you will notice some of the same faces showing up at each client. The fact that IT contractors are hired for specific technical skills means that the IT contract world can appear to be a very small world indeed. If the Rational Unified Process (RUP) just happens to be your thing, is it any surprise that the contractors you see hired alongside you for your next client's major RUP-adoption project are the same ones that were hired by your previous client – or the one before that?

It therefore pays to collect a few like-minded acquaintances along the way, who might be able to tip you off about the next suitable project or who might even be doing the hiring for it. I've hired my pseudo-colleagues on more than one occasion, and sometimes they've hired me.

This type of networking has now largely gone online in the form of social networks such as Facebook and…er…Facebook. Lest you think that Facebook is the only social network, let me tell you that the LinkedIn network at www.linkedin.com is perhaps *the place* for IT contractors and other professionals to link together. While your direct acquaintances may not have opportunities for you, their acquaintances might. And don't forget that the "six degrees of separation" means you're only five links away from Bill Gates or Steve Jobs!

Participation in Forums

What better way is there of showing off some of your skills and picking up some passing trade than by participating in technical forums? Suppose you have a passion for a relatively obscure technology such as Yahoo! Pipes, and you don't see many of those jobs advertised on the job sites. What you do know is that everyone who visits the Yahoo! Pipes message boards at http://discuss.pipes.yahoo.com/ is specifically interested in this technology and may be looking for a solution based on the technology. So why not help out on the forum by expertly answering a few of the questions posed by other users? But don't forget to conclude your responses with a subtle 'signature' containing your website address and a hint to contact you for further assistance. Like this one:

```
Shane Sekuloski, Technology Expert For Hire
www.shanesekuloski.com
```

This idea is perhaps more applicable to those of you who see yourselves as proper 'freelancers' rather than pseudo-employed 'contractors', and so is the next idea.

Freelancing Web Sites

Some of you might admit to yourselves (even if not to the HMRC) that you are in fact employees-in-contractors-clothing.

Others of you may have turned to contracting out of a genuine desire to become properly freelance: to have a completely free choice of who you work for, where, and when, or so that you can work predominantly from home.

Some of you might like to do a bit of both – regular contracting interspersed with true freelancing – as a lifestyle choice and to keep Her Majesty's IR35 inspectors at bay.

You won't find too much genuine 'freelance' work advertised on the job sites mentioned previously, but you can find other web sites, notably www.elance.com and www.freelancer.com, that are specifically geared towards freelance projects. They allow potential 'employers' (not in the legal sense) to post details of their projects and they allow freelancers like you to bid on those projects. These web sites take a percentage fee from the mutually-agreed price of the project, but they usually also provide an escrow facility that helps smooth the employer-to-freelancer payment process.

While this kind of web site would be of no particular use to a plumber who needs to be physically present to do a job, it is certainly possible to find a project poster (who could be anywhere in the world) for whom you can develop some software or write a report and deliver it electronically via email.

Advertising

I have known contractors who, upon setting up their limited companies, have then gone right ahead and advertised their Software Consultancy Business in the Yellow Pages. I'm not sure how effective this has been for those one-man-bands, and I would certainly shy away from any form of pay-for advertising, but I know that it can be useful to have some form of standing advertisement... in the form of a web site.

Some of the work-generation ideas discussed above and below depend on you directing your potential clients to a web page where they can find out more about you.

If you're not up to the task of cutting some hard-core HTML code despite your credentials as an IT professional, you will find that there are many easy ways to create a web site. For example, Google's blogging facility at www.blogger.com allows you to create a blog with up to ten additional freestanding web pages. That's sufficient for displaying your CV, a list of completed projects or clients, and (most importantly) your contact information all on separate pages.

Think Outside the Box

You will increase your chances of finding work, and of finding a diverse range of work and clients, if you employ as many different strategies as you can; the strategies outlined above plus some others that you can devise if you "think outside the box".

Note that by diversifying across clients and projects you increase your chances of falling outside the IR35 legislation, but be careful not to fall into the trap of avoiding a single big-paying client that would provide a more lucrative income even within the IR35 regime. As they say (paraphrased) in investment circles: don't let the tax-avoidance tail wag the 'wise investment' dog.

One way you can think laterally about advertising your services is by adding a signature that will appear automatically at the foot of every email you send. Almost all email programs allow you to do this, and your signature could look something like this (not literally, of course):

```
Shane Sekuloski, IT Contract Consultant for the Finance Industry
www.shanesekuloski.com
```

This is a subtle, incidental form of networking that will not yield immediate or easily identifiable results; but it costs you nothing to implement and "every little helps" when it comes to reminding people who you are and what you do.

By their very nature, outside-the-box techniques may not be immediately obvious – or else they'd be inside the box. So I can't provide you with a definitive list, but I can share with you one more example that may not be immediately obvious. It's Tony's Story.

Tony's Story

Tony was an IT consultant with a passion for writing; a passion that he satisfied initially by submitting articles for publication by online and print journals. This in itself provided him with another avenue for "getting his name out there" via the 'author bio' that most of the journal editors allowed him to include at the end of each article.

But Tony had bigger plans: he wanted to become a proper 'book' author. Not romantic fiction or anything like that; but books on IT topics. After having his work published by some big-name publishers (think 'Wiley'), and after taking the reins himself by self-publishing, and after achieving good reviews and ratings on Amazon, he discovered just how difficult it was actually to make money in the book publishing business. But he also learned something else.

This experience taught Tony just how effective his publishing efforts could be as a tactic for finding work and subsequently landing the job. He soon came to regard his books' product pages on Amazon as no-cost one-page subtle advertising slots for displaying his talents; advertising slots that could be viewed by thousands of people who he knew would have a direct interest – and possibly a project need – in the subject areas covered by the books. He also discovered that when he mentioned at interview the fact that he had "written the book on the subject" he was able to land almost every role he applied for.

We don't all have a passion or talent for writing, so I don't expect you to take this story so literally that you immediately put pen to paper – or fingers to keyboard. It's just an example of how inventive you can be when it comes to finding novel ways of promoting your talents and / or your business.

You will no doubt have noted the final statement about Tony: That "he was able to land almost every role he applied for", and this is the subject of the next chapter: Landing the Job.

the
Quick & Easy Guide
to **IT Contracting**
in the **UK**

3 – Landing the Job

Once you have found the perfect contract, you then need to try your best to actually *land the job*.

Your Application

When you apply for a contract role, this will generally be by submitting your up-to-date CV to the agency that advertised the role. Where possible, I would always include a 'covering letter' (these days usually in the form of an email) that grabs the agent's attention and which encourages him or her to read through your formal CV. Keep your 'covering email' short and sweet like this:

```
Dear Ms. Agent,

Please find my CV enclosed in relation to the contract role XYZ
that you advertised. It sounds right up my street, having just
successfully implemented a very similar project, and I am
available immediately for interview / to start work.

I look forward to discussing this role with you.

Shane Sekuloski, tel: 01234 567890
```

Expect the agent to call you to discuss the role in more detail, usually after having read through your attached CV but often (if you used the right form of words) a lot sooner than you might expect. In the cutthroat world of contract recruitment, each agency will be keen to be the first to put its suitable candidates in front of the client – so if you've got the right skills and you said the right things then they won't hang about.

On the other hand, agents receive hundreds of CVs, so there is no guarantee that you will hear back within a day – or at all. If you don't hear back within a day, don't be afraid to follow up with a call to the agent the next day. You have little to lose, and at the very least it might help nudge your CV towards the top of the queue by keeping you fresh in the agent's mind.

Your CV

Before you fire off your application as described above, you will need to make sure that your CV is up to scratch. While some contractors have a one-size-fits-all CV, I prefer to maintain a core CV that I adapt subtly for each job application so as to emphasise the skills and personal attributes that are particularly relevant to the role.

The generally recommended layout for your CV, which should be no more than 1-2 pages of clean presentation (nothing fancy) with bold headings, is something like this:

Personal Details

Your name, address, date-of-birth, and contact details (which may be removed by the agency prior to forwarding your CV to the client)

Education & Qualifications

A list of your academic qualifications and the institutions that awarded them, concentrating on the most recent / highest level qualifications. Also note that the client will be more interested in your Microsoft Certified Professional (MCP) status than your degree in art.

Technical Skills

As a contractor who will be hired primarily or his / her technical skills, it is important to list the technologies in which you have proficiency; such a .NET, Java, UML, Microsoft Solutions Framework. This will help the agency's computer or the client's eye to 'filter in' your CV as a potential match. Don't go overboard on this list, and only list those technologies in which you have genuine proficiency that you can demonstrate or back up with a good story.

Previous Contracts & Employment

Once your CV has been filtered into the pile of potential matches, this will become the most important section because the client will want to know about the real work you have done with real clients. Present your contracts and employments in reverse chronological order with a description of each role written in prose. Clients will be wary of any gaps in this work history – in case you spent a year in prison – so try to say something for every year of your working life. It's okay if you spent six months without a contract as long as you were writing a book, or doing some relevant demonstrable freelance work, or studying for a certification, or even trekking through the arctic.

Other Skills & Personal Interests

In theory this section should be less relevant for a potential contractor than for a potential permanent staff member, but many clients will nonetheless want to see that you are a well-rounded team-playing individual. It's a good idea to mention that you became fluent in Finnish while trekking the arctic, but probably not such a good idea to draw attention to your penchant for cross-dressing.

References

I'm not a big fan of references in CVs because they are easily circumvented (by asking one of your senior contractor friends to provide one) and because you won't want to keep asking your previous clients to support you in your search for your next contract. But many clients insist on references, and some agencies won't take your CV without them. My best advice is to have some referees at hand, but in your CV to simply state that "references can be provided on request". You really don't want your previous employers to be contacted until you're pretty sure you've got a good chance of landing the job.

While I prefer to write and layout my CV in my own style, some agencies and job sites enforce a particular structure which may be different from the one just outlined and which helps then collate your skills in their databases. The downside to an imposed CV structure is that it can encourage you to compose 'lists' of your skills rather than writing in prose about the real world projects and experiences that make you stand out. But if a particular structure is imposed, you'll have to abide by it if you want a shot at landing the job.

The usual advice about writing your CV applies, and I really don't need to tell you that it should be spell-checked and ideally read through by a friend or colleague prior to submission. However, do keep in mind that in the competitive world of IT contract recruitment it is often the early bird that catches the worm. So don't hang about.

CV Submission Tip: When you register and submit your CV for the first time to one of the job sites or agencies, you might notice agents call you quite soon because your CV is flagged as 'new'. You might be able to push yourself to the top of the queue every couple of weeks by removing and resubmitting your CV.

The Interview

Before you attend an interview, you should do some research by at least visiting the client company's web site. You will make a much better impression if you already know something about the client's products, services, and (ideally) projects. A few years ago when the contract market was awash with NHS IT projects, it wasn't too difficult to find out what the government-sponsored over-arching initiative was all about... simply by reading the news. Your mission at interview – should you choose to accept it – is to show how *your abilities* fit the *project needs*. You won't be able to do this if you don't actually what know the project needs are; so if you don't know – ask the agency.

When it comes to your interview technique, I'm not too keen on dispensing reams of advice that will have you so paranoid about your body language (are you sitting up straight?) or physical appearance (did you get a haircut?) that you forget the important stuff. In any case, those things should be obvious unless this is the first job interview of any kind that you have attended.

What is important is that you turn up in plenty of time rather than arriving flustered and late. If you're early, you can always drive around the block a few times or have a coffee in the nearby café until the allotted time – but be careful not to spill it all over your new shirt! Despite your prompt attendance, the client might keep you waiting either as a juvenile attempt to display some power over the interviewee, or simply because they're not as organised as you. Take this in good spirit as part of the game, because you can afford to indulge the client who will ultimately be paying you a lot of money.

No two interviews are exactly alike, but I have found contract interviews usually to be less formal than interviews for permanent positions. You are more likely to simply chat with the project manager, and less likely to be set a personality test by the Human Resources manager.

If you are presented with an opportunity to do something interactive like leaping (not literally) to a whiteboard to draw a diagram, take this opportunity as a welcome distraction from the more usual question-and-answer duelling.

If you've written a book or published an article on the subject at hand, take a copy along to the interview if only to place it on the desk in front of you (next to your CV) as an invitation for the interviewer(s) to ask:

"Oh, what's that you've brought along?"

This will help put the interview under your control, so that you're more relaxed and less stressed than if you were being 'interrogated' with a list of formulaic interview questions. And it will help you to stand out from the crowd.

To talk about money, or not to talk about money, that is the question. While some clients may be as keen as you are to figure out how much percentage the agent is taking from what they're paying and what you're receiving, the prevailing advice is to not bring up the subject of your pay rate unless the client does; and in any event, the agent won't like it. Don't feel too bad if it subsequently turns out that the agent took a bigger slice of the pie than you or the client would have liked; it's something you can address when your contract comes up for renewal and you have established a good working relationship with the client that the agent will not want to upset for the sake of a few percentage points.

As a contractor you will likely attend more interviews over the course of your career than you would as a regular employee, if only because you'll likely be moving between clients more often than you would have changed jobs. You should become quite seasoned in the art of being interviewed, and you'll learn to recognise the "buy signals" that the interviewers give out subconsciously to tell you that you've got the job.

This leads me to my final, and arguably most important, piece of advice about attending interviews:

Once you've sold it… shut up!

When you feel confident that you've pretty much landed the job, anything more that you say can only lessen your chances of being hired. So while you shouldn't actually run out of the door, it might be a good idea to cut out the post-interview small-talk that reveals your previously hidden unsavoury interests.

Think Outside the Box

Most of the agencies, job sites, and books like this one will tell you about the tried-and-tested 'conventional' way of landing a job: write a good CV, dress well for the interview, and so on.

It is good advice, no doubt, but it won't work in every situation when you're up against many well-dressed applicants with well-written CVs. It could be that in some situations the interviewers are looking for something different in order to help them choose the right candidate.

I know a contractor who, when he turned up at interview and was invited to read through his CV, said:

"I haven't brought my CV with me because I don't think it shows off my achievements as well as these artefacts (some previous project documentation, and a published article) that I have brought to show you instead."

After an initial look of shock that this impetuous candidate had refused the offer of talking through his CV as was expected, the interviewers exclaimed that in fact they were looking for an original thinker who could take on the project with minimal guidance. And they gave him the job!

This unconventional approach will likely be too 'high risk' for your first few interview attempts, but for more seasoned candidates who know how to read an interviewing panel and are up against a large number of carbon copy candidates... it might just work.

Be quirky but not combative, and remember above all that *personality counts*. Your client knows that they can train someone technically, but not socially!

Negotiating the Rate

Once the agent tells you that the client wants to get you on board, it's time to finalise the rate you will be paid, and this will usually be a daily rate or in some cases an hourly rate.

The agent will often have teased your minimum acceptable rate out of you at the outset before even submitting your CV to the client, so don't be surprised if this is the rate you are offered. The agent might offer you a little more than what he has determined to be your baseline rate, so as to appear to have acted in *your interests* when negotiating with the client; but it's just as likely that he could afford to reduce his otherwise oversized commission just a little in order to create this win-win illusion.

The initial advertisement may well have indicated a rate or rate-range for the role; and it's useful to try and spot the same job advertised by one than one agent. Not necessarily so that you can pursue it through the agent who apparently offers the best rate, but so that you can get a feel for the 'true' rate that is on offer irrespective of the differences in agents' commissions.

You can try asking for a rate higher than the baseline rate you indicated initially (as long as it's within the advertised range) on the basis of "what you learned about the role during the interview" or on the basis of what an outstanding candidate you are, but there's not much point in saying that you need a higher rate in order to feed your children or to pay your mortgage. Those are not the agent's problems.

As with any negotiation, you can only really play hardball if you are willing to walk away. More seasoned contractors with big bank balances might try a do-or-die approach that lands them either a big pay-out or a disgruntled agent.

Although not advisable in your early days of contracting, you'll learn not to worry too much about upsetting the recruitment agents. They can be very fickle; one minute lambasting you for wasting their time (i.e. not accepting the low rate / high agent commission on offer) and the next minute being incredibly friendly when they realise you are the best candidate on their books for the latest client contract that has just come in. Don't take anything too personally; it's only business… and money.

My final piece of advice for negotiating your rate is to think about the long-term picture as well as the possible short-term gain. I know of at least one contractor who took a slightly lower rate in 2003 to work on his first .NET contract rather than be typecast forever as a Java programmer. His short-term pain – hey, it was still a good rate – ensured that he remained 'in demand' for many years to come.

Getting Accommodated and Starting Work

Unless you're based in London, where you may find many clients within an acceptable commuting distance, your life as a contractor is likely to be a life away from home. So once you've landed the work you'll have to find a place to live while you do the job.

Be careful not to commit to a six month lease on a house when starting work with a brand new client on a contract that specifies a one month notice period. It may be wise to live in a hotel for the first month while you find your feet and get them firmly under the table, and while you are waiting to bank you first month's payment.

As with any business, in your contracting business you will learn that "cash is king". So don't go spending it or committing to spend it before you've actually earned it. And don't be tempted to live the high life now that you are set to earn hundreds of pounds per day. In most cases the costs of you traveling from your home base in Cheshire to your client in Northumberland, and the costs of you being accommodated there, are your problem; not the agency's and not the client's. Only by thinking Travelodge rather than Savoy you will be able to bank the excess profits that will help you through the tough times when you're 'between contracts' or are too ill to work.

You didn't think that IT contracting was going to provide you with a champagne lifestyle, did you?

There is another good reason for not committing to long-term accommodation at the outset: you may simply not have time to do so. Unlike a traditional 'permanent' employment that takes a while to come to fruition, in the contracting world it is not unknown to be offered a job on Friday afternoon and be expected to turn up for work on Monday morning. This could result in a frantic exchange of contracts by email over the weekend, so make sure you can be contacted easily.

Even if you are afforded the more usual week or two of grace between landing the job and turning up for work, it will be a busy time with plenty of exchanging of information – including contracts, forms of identification, bank details – between you and the agency.

After all this frenetic activity to get you on site as soon as possible, don't be surprised if you are greeted on the first day with no desk, no computer, and pretty much nothing to do for the first few days – but don't count on this! Try to make yourself as useful as you can from the outset, and take comfort in the fact that you should still be paid your daily rate merely for showing up on time.

There's something else you need to do before going on site for your first contract role, or a soon as possible thereafter, which is to set yourself up as a business...

the
Quick & Easy Guide
to **IT Contracting**
in the **UK**

4 – Setting Up Your Business

In order ultimately to get paid for the work you do under contract, and to be assessed for the right amount of tax, you will need to have some kind of business structure in place. In this chapter we'll look at the possible business structures.

I'll tell you what I understand to be true, but I stress at the outset that I am not an authorised business- or tax-advisor. So do your own research, and don't come crying to me if you make the wrong choice!

PAYE Umbrella Company

The simplest mechanism for engaging with the contract agency is through an Umbrella Company, because then you don't need to set up your own business at all. You simply become an 'employee' of the umbrella company, which submits invoices to the agency on your behalf, which deals with all the accounting and tax issues, and which simply pays you a salary plus expenses.

The umbrella company won't tell you which clients you have to work for, or which agencies you have to work through, so you retain control over your career choices while leaving them to handle the paperwork. As an employee of the umbrella company rather than the end client, you should be able to claim travel and accommodation expenses that would be denied to you when traveling to your "normal place of work" as a direct client employee.

There are some disadvantages, like the fact that you need to maintain yet another relationship – with the umbrella company as well as with the agency and the end client – but this form of business arrangement may be suitable for you at least for your first contract.

Your tax arrangements would be no different from how they are now, since you would submit a personal Self-Assessment tax return annually to Her Majesty's Revenue and Customs (HMRC) just like you do now.

You can find a list of umbrella companies at:

http://www.contractoruk.com/directory/umbrella_companies.html

As you research these companies you may also encounter umbrella-alternative companies that promise to pay out a larger proportion of your gross contract value (even than your own limited company) by employing clever tax strategies. I can't vouch for these companies, but I can tell you that the best piece of advice I ever read in relation to these companies was (paraphrased):

"If you want to sleep well at night while using one of these companies, put about 30% of your income away in a savings account and do not touch it for 7 years. After seven years you can start taking it out knowing you have got away with it."

The point being made here is that ultimately *you* are on the line for any penalties or unpaid tax in the event that these schemes do not live up to their promises... or if turn out to be not entirely legitimate. Under normal circumstances, the HMRC can only challenge you as far back as six years full years, which is why you should be in the clear by the seventh year.

Remember that my words of caution relate to the umbrella-alternative companies and not the vanilla umbrella companies.

Sole Trader

The next easiest route from an administration perspective is to set yourself up as the kind of one-man-band business known as a sole trader.

Unlike the limited company route that we'll discuss shortly, a sole trader doesn't need to register the business at Companies House and doesn't need to set up a Pay As Your Earn (PAYE) arrangement in order to take a salary. You just tell the HMRC that you are 'in business' and you pay tax on your business profits minus your legitimate business expenses. You pay National Insurance at a weekly flat rate plus some additional NI as a proportion of your profits.

Since you have to do *some* additional administration for accounting and tax purposes, you may conclude that you might as well go the whole hog and attain limited company status; especially when you consider that as a sole trader you are personally liable for the business's debts as well as potentially having your home and other assets on the line in the case of an adverse law suit.

Professional Indemnity (PI) insurance and other business insurances may be even more important for a sole trader than for a limited company director, since you don't have the option of simply declaring the company bankrupt (and walking away) without declaring yourself bankrupt in the process.

Finally, you may find that agencies and clients are less willing to hire you as a sole trader than as a director / employee operating through a limited company.

Partnership, and Limited Liability Partnership (LLP)

It is possible for you to band together with one of more like-minded individuals, or with your spouse, to form a business partnership.

Traditional partnerships are similar to sole traders from a legal tax perspective in that the business has no separate independent existence from the partners, and all partners are personally and jointly liable for the business's debts. Each partner must submit a self-assessment tax return to the HMRC, and a 'nominated' partner submits one on behalf of the partnership as a whole.

The main drawback of a partnership is the lack of personal protection against business failure, which is a risk you are sharing with people you might not be able to trust absolutely, but this problem can be at least partly addressed by the Limited Liability Partnership (LLP).

Traditionally it was quite common for firms of accountants, lawyers, and business consultants to be incorporated as partnerships rather than limited companies. A Limited Liability Partnership (LLP) allows such firms to retain the partnership nature of their organisations while enjoying a degree of *limited liability* status. In reality it is unlikely that you will incorporate as an LLP, so I have mentioned this option merely in the interests of completeness.

The most popular form of business for an IT contractor has been, and most probably continues to be the...

Limited Company

A limited company is an entity that has a separate legal existence from its members. It means that the members can change (or die) without affecting the status of the company, and any business contracts and law suits are the responsibility of the company rather than the members. If the business fails, you don't have to fail with it. If the business gets big, you can sell it.

Aside from the protection that *limited liability* affords you, many contractors choose this form of incorporation in order to optimise the payment of the business income out to its members (i.e. you) in the most tax-efficient way via some combination of salary, pension contributions, and dividends.

It's beyond the scope of this guide to tell you what the optimal tax-minimisation strategy is, and in any case I'm not qualified to do so, so you'll have to talk to an accountant. But I can steer you in the right direction by telling you that many contractors pay the minimum salary necessary to secure their national insurance benefits while taking the majority of their income in the form of dividends that are taxed at a lower rate than PAYE salary. When deciding to go down this route, do keep the following things in mind:

- Some years ago the HMRC introduced the dreaded IR35 legislation in order to discourage employees-in-contractors-clothing from operating as one-man limited companies simply to perform these tax-minimisation tricks.

- Your annual PAYE P60 showing a modest salary of circa £7,500 per annum (the rest being paid out in dividends) won't get you very far through a mortgage application process unless you can also show several years' worth of company accounts that demonstrate just how well your business is doing financially.

- Your annual before-tax pension contributions may well be limited to a proportion of your salary, which means you'll be able to squirrel away less money tax-efficiently for your old age if you take a small salary.

On the assumption that I've not dissuaded you from incorporating as a limited company, you'll now want to know how to set one up.

Setting Up Your Limited Company

The first thing you'll need is another person, because, as a minimum, a limited company requires two 'officers' to act as the Director and the Company Secretary. Like many IT contractors, you might decide to appoint your wife as the second officer – well, at least it will stop her worrying about you running off with your secretary.

Note for female contractors: I'm not being sexist here. The same joke applies to you when you appoint your husband as your company secretary.

In many cases, this appointment of a second officer is merely 'ceremonial' in the sense that you may never actually ask your company secretary to perform any administrative functions for the company; but this does not mean that the appointment of a company secretary should be taken too lightly. Company officers have certain responsibilities and obligations, even if they don't exercise them, and these are outlined in a booklet that Companies House (http://www.companieshouse.gov.uk/) should send you when you incorporate.

The easiest way to set up your company is to engage a company formation agent, who, for a small fee of a few hundred pounds, will draw up the legal documents including a

Memorandum of Association and *Articles of Association* and will register your company with Companies House.

You will need to let the HMRC know about your company, so that they can prompt you to submit a corporation tax return at the end of your company's 'tax year' and so that they can set up a PAYE account for the collection of any income tax and national insurance contributions due on the salaries you pay your employees. Those employees will be you, and possibly (but not necessarily) your company secretary.

Setting up your Accounts and Payroll

You will most likely want to engage with an accountant who will tell you what day-to-day book-keeping you need to do so that he (or she) can prepare your tax returns and annual accounts at the end of each year. Some accountants and online service providers will even handle the basic book-keeping chores if you simply send them a pile of receipts and invoices each month.

Note that for small companies – which means yours unless you are expecting to turnover more than £2m or employ tens of people – you do not have to prepare 'audited' accounts, and you are allowed to submit annual accounts directly to the HMRC and Companies House yourself without the help of an accountant… if you're up to the task.

If you're doing the accounts or at least the basic book-keeping yourself, you will probably be using an accounting software package such as the one offered by Sage, or you might decide to subscribe to their Sage One online accountancy solution described at:

http://www.sage.co.uk/pages/products/sage-one-accounts/sage-one-accounts-overview.html

Most accountancy software packages and solutions will record your sales and purchases, will allow you to generate invoices, and will produce account statements in the form of a Profit & Loss statement and a Balance Sheet. They won't run your Pay As You Earn (PAYE) payroll.

To run your payroll you will need a separate payroll software package such as Sage Payroll; or you can sign up with a third-party payroll agency. Ask your accountant about this, if you have one, but as a small company with only one or two 'employees' you may find that the HMRC's own Basic PAYE Tools to be perfectly sufficient. You can find out more about this at:

http://www.businesslink.gov.uk/bdotg/action/layer?topicId=10 86857322

Your Company Bank Account

When you incorporate your business as a limited company it will strike you as obvious that you will need a 'company' bank account. Even as a sole trader whose business profits are taxed alongside personal income, you would benefit from a dedicated bank account that keeps your business finances separate from your personal finances. In this context you can also benefit from looking like a more professional outfit by applying for a bank account with a *trading name,* so that you can bank cheques made out to your business and so that you can write cheques labelled with:

```
Shane Sekuloski
T/A Sekuloski Consultancy Services
```

Just because you have a trading name, it doesn't mean you have a limited company, so in this case you would only be able to bank cheques made out to "Sekuloski Consultancy Services" and would be unable to bank cheques made out to "Sekuloski Consultancy Services Ltd."

Whether as a sole trader or a limited company, you should find many banks offering business accounts that are fee-free for the first year; after which you will have to pay small bank charges for all the transactions going into and out of the account. You will need to provide some documentation in support of your business bank account application, for example your limited company's *certificate of incorporation.*

As an IT contractor you shouldn't need any start-up capital in the form of a loan from the bank, and in our post-financial-crisis world you may be unlikely to get any. Just open the account with a couple of thousand pounds of your own money.

If you intend to provide services wholly or partly on a true freelance basis – i.e. not for and end-client via an agency – then you will find a PayPal account invaluable as a destination for payments from directly-engaged clients around the world. Sign up for a PayPal account for your business at www.paypal.co.uk, and keep this separate from your personal PayPal account.

Registering for VAT

You can register your business for VAT as soon as you set it up, which will allow you to claim back the VAT on the new 'business' laptop you just bought. Or you can wait until your business turnover approaches the VAT threshold of (currently) £73,000.

Most IT contractors will want to register for VAT, because the client or agency will pay VAT in addition to the pay rate that you agreed, yet you will be able to claim back the VAT that you pay out on your traveling and equipment expenses. So it's something of a no-brainer.

Some freelancers may not want the additional administrative overhead of VAT invoicing and accounting if:

- Most of your clients are individuals who are not registered for VAT themselves, for whom your prices would effectively be 20% higher.

- You work mainly from home with your only expense being a single laptop computer.

- Your 'lifestyle' business – i.e. one that you run for an easy life rather than to make as much money as possible – turns over significantly less than the VAT threshold.

If I know IT contractors at all, I know that they will provide services mainly to other VAT-registered businesses, they will travel extensively, and they will try to make as much money as possible. Hence, they will be registered for VAT.

Next Steps

You've found the right contract (chapter 2), you've landed the job (chapter 3), and you've set up your business (this chapter). So now it's time for you to actually *do the job* by working on site.

the
Quick & Easy Guide
to **IT Contracting**
in the **UK**

5 – Working on Site

Now it's time for you to turn up at the client site and actually *do the job*. It goes without saying that you should turn up on time, so I won't try to patronise you with that piece of advice.

Note that if you're intending to work from home on an entirely freelance basis, this chapter will be of lesser interest to you. But it's worth reading all the same.

Your First Few Days

As hinted in Chapter 3, it's not unknown that during your first couple of days you will be offered nothing to do and no equipment with which to (not) do it. Alternatively you'll be directed to the desk that has just been vacated by the last guy who did your job, with a PC scavenged from under someone else's desk and an instruction for you to plug it all together yourself, and with a big pile of project background information for you to read through while your new boss – er, client – thinks up something useful for you to do.

In order to function in your new work environment you'll need a login ID for the client's computer network and most likely a security pass to get you in and out of the office. If my experiences are anything to go by, it will take the IT and HR department a few days to get their acts together on these two counts, so you'll be accessing the network using the ID of one of your new-found colleagues and using their security pass to go to the toilet.

Use your downtime productively and at least *look busy*, even if you're busy tying up the loose ends with the agency that you didn't have time to finalise before starting work.

If you're stuck for ideas, here's something you may have forgotten to put in place, which is relevant to the fact that you are now working *on site*:

Liability Insurance

Although I've heard of very few cases where this has actually happened, there is a theoretical possibility of you tripping someone up or dropping a piece of expensive equipment while working on site – and being sued for it. It is advisable, therefore, for IT contractors to take out some form of Public Liability insurance to protect themselves in the unlikely event that they cause damage to persons or property.

Similarly, although on most IT contracts you will be following the client's instructions rather than providing 'professional advice' as such, most contractors have in place some form of

Professional Indemnity insurance that covers the costs of defending an action brought against you for giving bad advice.

You may regard the chances of ever making a claim on such insurances to be negligible, and you may be content to simply "shut up shop" on your limited company in the event of being presented with an unaffordable law suit. As a sole trader you would not have this option, and even as a limited company director you may find that having sufficient insurance in place is a condition of your contract with the agency and / or client.

There are other forms of insurance you might also consider including office insurance (to cover your own computer equipment and premises) and employers' liability insurance (if you decide to expand to take on more staff).

A web search of the phrase "IT contractor insurance" will lead you to several providers offering all-in-one insurance packages specifically designed for IT contractors.

Office Politics

My advice on office politics is simple: don't get involved. You don't need to because this won't be a whole-of-life job in which you need to build your own empire. It sounds mercenary, but – while you will no doubt be loyal to your clients while working for them – you're really only doing it for the money. Just keep banking the cheques while the others fight it out.

A Lonely Life on the Road

I'm not joking when I say that your life as an IT contractor could turn out to be a lonely existence. Unless you are lucky enough to land a series of contracts that require *your skills* in *your neck of the woods*, there's a good chance that you will be spending extended periods away from your home, your family, and your regular friends. This can be both exciting and boring.

One strategy for dealing with it is to get involved with the client social scene; whether this is hitting the city bars or joining the five-a-side football team. The client's own staff and the other contractors – who would otherwise be just as bored as you – will in most cases be willing to admit you to their social circles; at least for a 'trial period'.

The problem comes with those contracts where the client is based on a campus or industrial estate (rather than a city centre location) where there are no bars nearby and where the predominantly 'permanent' staff members go home each evening to their spouses and families.

Contractor Tip: If you are offered a contract in a major city like London, jump at it! Not only will the fast-paced financial (or similar) environment leave you anything but bored, but also it's a great springboard for gaining exposure to international clients and organisations.

In the event of landing a rural or industrial campus-based client, let me suggest another strategy:

Do more work!

I don't mean take a second employment-like contract or wait tables in the evenings (although it's an idea). I mean write that book that you knew you always had in you, or log onto the freelancing web sites at www.elance.com and www.freelancer.com to find small projects that you can do entirely remotely. It will help take your mind off the tedium of the long evening hours spent locked away in your hotel room or – let's face it – in a corner of the hotel bar.

By overdosing on work and maximising your income during your 'captive' time away from home, you might buy yourself some additional time to utilise during your next extended-holiday between contracts.

If all else fails, get a season ticket for the local cinema and become a film buff. If you've never done it before, you might find it a little odd visiting the cinema alone, but you'll get used to it; just as you'll get used to the phrase "Will anyone be joining Sir?" whenever you visit a restaurant alone.

However it turns out, you can keep reminding yourself of one thing: you're being paid a lot of money! Aren't you?

Timesheets

We'll look at this again in the next chapter on getting paid, but, in order to get paid at all, you will need to complete timesheets on a weekly basis. You'll get them authorised by the client, and then you'll submit them to the agency.

This used to be a paper process whereby you would carry around a ream of pro-forma timesheets on which you would scribble in your hours worked each week. You would try to track down your client 'boss' on a Friday afternoon so as to get your attendance signed off before the weekend, and then you'd drop your timesheet into one of the agency-supplied postal envelopes. Sometimes you would fail to obtain a client signature until the following week, and sometimes you would find that the client representative would expect you to more-or-less beg each time for them to sign off the timesheet – even if you'd been on your best behaviour all week.

In most if not all cases, this process has now been computerised. The agency will give you a login ID for their web-based timesheet program, and, as soon as you have submitted your hours online, the client representative will be emailed with an invitation to authorise the timesheet for payment. No more embarrassing face-to-face encounters in order to get your worked signed off – phew!

Many clients will also have their own internal timesheet systems that have nothing to do with you getting paid, but which they use in order to discover how much time their staff members (including the contractors) spend on each project and in meetings.

In some cases I have even known there to be an end client who retained the services of a single recruitment agency who then sourced contract staff through other agencies (including the one you have been hired by) thereby creating a tripartite timesheet arrangement. In this set-up you would find yourself completing timesheets for two different agencies plus the client. Usually the various parties see sense and reach a compromise on a simpler arrangement.

As you complete your 'hourly' timesheets, note that on the majority of contracts you will be paid a 'day rate' by which any additional hours worked will not count except by prior agreement. You won't be paid for overtime, so within reason, don't do it! Most clients and agencies will allow a degree of flexibility whereby, if you find yourself staying late for an important meeting, they will allow you to record fewer hours the next day as long as the weekly total equals the 37.5 or 40 hours-per-week that you are contracted for.

--

So – you've got set up, you've managed to do your job without getting sued, you've whiled away the lonely evening hours, and you've completed your timesheets. Now it's time to *get paid*, which unfortunately also means paying tax. Every silver lining has a cloud, eh?

the
Quick & Easy Guide
to **IT Contracting**
in the **UK**

6 – Getting Paid and Paying Tax

In this chapter I'll address the issue of getting paid for the work you do on-site as a regular contractor operating via an agency. Unlike the previous chapter, I won't assume you to be entirely site-bound, and so I'll also consider the possibility that you'll be taking payments for additional freelance work or private direct-to-client projects.

Raising Invoices

In order to get paid for the work you have done, you will need to raise an invoice. In the past you would have generated an invoice using your book-keeping program (such as Sage) or you would have used a Microsoft Word document template to create an invoice. You would have dropped this invoice into an envelope along with your completed timesheets and you would have posted it out to the agency.

These days you're more likely to save your invoice as an electronic Portable Document Format (PDF) file on your computer, and email it. Or you might find that the agency has a self-invoicing facility whereby submission of your online timesheet(s) will trigger the generation of an internal invoice on your behalf.

If your business is registered for VAT, the VAT amount should be added to your invoice over-and-above the amount you are expecting to be paid. Assuming a VAT rate of 20%, your VAT-registered business would invoice for £1,200 – broken out as £1,000 for services provided plus £200 for VAT – whereas your non-VAT-registered business would simply invoice £1,000 for services provided.

If you invoice for the higher amount, the additional £200 is not yours to keep, sorry, and at the end of the month or quarter you'll have to pay it to the HMRC minus any VAT you have incurred on business purchases you have made.

Receiving the Money

The agency will have asked for your business bank account details when you signed your contract, so the amounts due to you should be deposited automatically into your bank account according to the agency's schedule.

In some rare cases an agency or your direct client (where no agency is involved) might send you a cheque which you'll deposit into your company bank account in the usual way using a paying-in slip.

Special Notes for Freelancers

If you're doing pure 'freelance' work, in addition to or instead of agency contract work, things will work somewhat differently.

By far the best way of raising invoices and receiving payments from clients all around the world in various currencies is via a PayPal account that you can set up at www.paypal.com. Theoretically is possible to run your PayPal account rather like a bank account, taking payments in and making payments out, but it is more usual to use PayPal as a staging post for incoming payments en route to your real bank account. My advice would be to maintain a cash 'float' in your PayPal account and to transfer surplus funds periodically into your bank account.

If you bid for projects on one of the freelancing web sites such as elance.com or freelancer.com you will find that they operate a two-stage escrow facility which allows your clients to deposit their money (so you know they can pay) and later release the funds for the work you have done. Any released funds will be added to your freelancing account balance, from where you can transfer them to your regular bank account or your PayPal account.

> *Freelancing Tip:* Upon acceptance of your bid on a project, invite your client to structure the project as a series of milestones rather than one big payment. Not only will this give your client confidence that they will only have to commit to, and pay for, work that is actually completed, but also it will ensure that you will be paid *at least something* in the event that a dispute occurs somewhere down the line. It's a win-win situation because neither of you will be disadvantaged by an all-or-nothing payment scenario.

What if you don't get paid?

It's all well and good talking about getting paid, but what if you don't get paid?

The first thing to do is to find out why you've not been paid, and to ask if there's anything you need to do. Call or email the agency and say something along the lines of:

"I was wondering why I've not been paid as expected. Did you receive my invoice / timesheets okay, or is there anything else you need from me in order to make the payment?"

They will be obliged to tell you what you need to do in order to resolve the problem, or to admit that the payment has been delayed despite you having fulfilled your obligations. Ask them for a date by which the payment will now be made, and providing it's in the near future (i.e. not "in six months' time") simply wait for this date to pass.

I know you'll be keen to maintain a good relationship, and not to bite the hand that feeds, but once the promised payment date has passed… it's time to ratchet up the pressure to pay. One advantage of working through an agency is that you can yell at your agent without upsetting the end client at all. As long as you have a good relationship with the client, *the agency won't fire you*! Furthermore, if the agent complains that they have "not yet been paid by the client" then your alarm bells should start to ring. Part of the 'added value' that an agency provides in exchange for a large slice of commission is to pay you in exchange for authorised timesheets irrespective of whether the client has paid up.

You're more likely to run into payment problems with small agencies and (if you deal direct) with small clients. They may well have cash-flow problems; but these are not your problem – so make getting your money a higher priority than sympathising with their plight.

Some small agencies and companies who are in financial difficulties might over-candidly explain to you that you are more likely to get paid if you give them time to pay, rather than driving them under with your demand to get paid. Don't fall for it! It won't be because of you alone that they go to the wall, so your only priority is to make sure that you get paid before they do go bust. And (I'm sorry to say) to make sure you get paid before their other contractors do. Remember this:

"It's the squeaky wheel that gets the oil!"

If you think that your agency or small client really is on the brink, then one of the most cost-effective ways of getting paid is to get a solicitor or online service provider to issue a "letter before action" that threatens (politely) to commence wind-up proceedings if your invoice is not paid within 7 days. It should cost you only about £10 if issued via an online debt recovery firm, and it will usually do the trick!

Believe it or not, I have heard of some small companies that routinely do not pay invoices until they have received an LBA. These companies usually don't last long.

Believe it or not, I have also heard of some very small contractors who have threatened to wind-up some very large companies!

Joking aside, if you do go down this route, keep it professional and not personal. You can show that you are serious about pursuing your payments without being nasty about it.

If you find yourself not being paid in a timely manner, there may be a temptation for you to threaten to 'down tools' until you are paid. In some cases this might work, for example: if an on-line journal editor asks you to write an article for their next edition, you might offer to do so as soon as they pay up for your previous unpaid submission.

If you're working a regular IT contract via an agency, the 'down tools' approach is likely to be counter-productive if in effect you are punishing the client for difficulties you are experiencing with the agency. Unless you have some other paid work to do, you have little to lose by continuing to work... for a while... until the payment problem is resolved. If your relationship with the end-client is good, a few well-timed hints that you are having payment problems with the agency could work wonders since the agent will not want to lose face with the client. And let's face it – if the agency or client is going to pay you £1000-or-not, it might as well be £2,000-or-not.

Paying Yourself, and Paying Tax

Once your company has been paid for the work you have done, you then need to decide how to pay the proceeds out to yourself – minus any tax due to the HMRC. How much you can pay yourself, and how much tax will be due as a consequence, will depend on whether you take the money from your company as a salary, as dividends, or as sole trader income.

There are several online calculators that will show you what difference it makes, and as an example I have run some numbers through the Dividends vs. Salary tool that you will find at:

http://www.uktaxcalculators.co.uk/dividend-vs-salary.php

The numbers I entered were as follows:

Tax Year: 2011 / 2012

Gross Company Profit: £62,000

(Day rate of £300 x 240 days = £72,000, take away £10,000 for travelling and accommodation expenses)

Sex: Male

Age: 37

Your numbers may be different. You might achieve a higher day rate or spend less on 'expenses', thereby achieving a higher gross profit. But it doesn't matter because what is important is how much of the *gross profit* you can take home as *net income*.

The results come out as follows:

- By operating as a **limited company** you could take home a *salary* of £7,475 plus a *net dividend* of £43,575.51 giving a total net income (after tax) of about **£48,000**. You would pay the equivalent of **22.58%** in (company + personal) tax.

- By taking the full amount from your limited company in the form of a **director's salary** (no dividends) your gross salary of £55,339.14 would be reduced to take-home pay of about **£38,700** thanks to a **37.57%** tax bill.

- By operating as a **sole trader** you would be able to take home almost **£43,500** of your £62,000 gross profit, after incurring a **29.84%** tax bill.

Clearly the most tax-efficient route to converting your *gross profits* into *net income* is to take a small salary and a large dividend from your limited company. But only if you can legitimately do so under the regime known as…

IR35

If there are four alphanumeric characters that strike fear into the hearts of IT contracts and other professional service providers, it's these four characters:

I – R – 3 – 5

The IR35 tax legislation was introduced by the UK Government in April 2000 in order to prevent IT contractors and other professionals from providing their services on an employment-like basis through their own limited companies merely as a means of avoiding tax and National Insurance by paying dividends rather than salary.

If the HMRC determines that you are effectively 'employed' by your end client, all of your income from that client will be treated for tax purposes to have been paid to you from your limited company in the form of salary – even if paid in part via dividends. And you'll be taxed accordingly.

Note that if the IR35 legislation applies to your contract(s), then, although you will be liable for higher income tax and National Insurance contributions, you will still benefit from the following concessions compared with regular employment:

- You can deduct a general 5% allowance from your income before calculating the IR35 liability.

- You can deduct your legitimate travel, accommodation, and other business expenses.

- You can deduct your pension contributions.

You might conclude that these concessions – along with the benefits of having 'limited liability' status – are in themselves better than being officially 'employed'. Nonetheless, you will be keen to ensure that your work falls outside of the IR35 regime.

If you are a genuine freelancer who supplies project 'deliverables' (e.g. reports or software) to many clients, sometimes simultaneously, from your own home of office, in your own good time, then you're on pretty safe ground.

If you work for a single client at their site for an extended period of time then you're not on such safe ground and you'll want to check how 'IR35-friendly' your contract is. You'll want to look out for clauses that address the following points:

Nature of Work and Schedules: describing projects or deliverables rather than on-going work.

Right of Control: such that the contractor rather than the client determines the method and manner of performance.

Substitution: the right for the contractor to provide a replacement person of equivalent ability.

Mutuality of Obligation: whereby each party's obligation extends only for the life of the contract, with further obligation necessitating a separate contract.

Termination: coinciding with the length of the contract rather than being on the basis of a 'notice period'.

Financial Risk: where the contractor must make good any substandard work at his (or her) own expense, or where sufficient professional indemnity insurance should be kept in force.

Payment terms: would ideally be on a fixed-price basis, and where based on hours worked (the usual case) any payments should be in response to invoices issued.

Exclusivity: should allow the contractor to maintain relationships with other clients.

Equipment and Premises: should not be restricted to those of the client when some tasks may be performed by the contractor at his own premises and / or using his own equipment.

Intention: should confirm that both parties (client and contractor) are independent businesses with no intention of creating an employment relationship.

Obviously you will be keener on some of these contract provisions than others, and you or the agency or the client might not want to agree on the inclusion of them all. Be realistic while understanding that the more such provisions are included, the merrier you'll be. And keep in mind that, whatever is stipulated in the contract, it should be representative of what is actually occurring on the ground.

Once you're sure you are on safe ground regarding IR35, or if you're willing to accept the more onerous tax treatment, you can relax! But not until you ensure that you're not operating through a limited company for the purposes of…

Income Splitting

There is another tax-saving initiative that many IT contractors and other similar professionals employed while operating as a limited company.

You make your non-working spouse a joint shareholder of the company and you pay her (although it might be him) a basic salary of £7,475 plus half of the dividends that you would have paid out entirely to yourself. Your spouse would pay no tax or national insurance on the salary and would pay a lower tax rate on the dividends than if you had taken the full amount of dividends yourself.

The test case of Arctic Systems vs. Inland Revenue (as it was called then) struck fear into the hearts of many IT contractors who were running similar tax-avoidance – but note, not tax-evasion – schemes until this case was thrown out by the House of Lords. Phew! But then the Government changed the law to 'outlaw' the practice anyway.

If your accountant recommends this kind of 'income splitting' arrangement, you might think twice about it. But note that there should be nothing wrong with paying your spouse a salary (and possibly even dividends) if s/he actually performs legitimate work for your business – and especially if they generate a substantial proportion of the business income.

In a nutshell: when it comes to having your spouse as a *sleeping partner*, make sure that this is in the 'personal' rather than 'business' sense!

7 – Summary of Tips, Tricks and Resources

My aim with this book was to make it a "quick & easy" guide to IT Contracting in the UK, and so in this chapter I present you with my quick & easy summary of the content.

Your contracting road map consists of five steps:

Finding Contract Work, outlined in **Chapter 2**

Landing the Job, outlined in **Chapter 3**

Setting Up Your Business (if you haven't done so already), outlined in **Chapter 4**

Working On Site, outlined in **Chapter 5**

Getting Paid and Paying Tax, outlined in **Chapter 6**

Here are my summaries of the key tips and tricks from each chapter:

Finding Contract Work

You can look for contract work on the three main IT contracting job sites or by using the one-stop-shop job search provided by the Contractor UK web site (see the Resources section below). As well as submitting your CV to contract agencies – and refreshing it periodically – you can network with like-minded professionals via social networks and online forums. To supplement your contract work, you might undertake additional freelance projects sourced through the freelancing web sites.

Landing the Job

To land the job you will need an attention-grabbing covering letter, a well-written CV, a good interview technique, and (perhaps most important) a good story that sets you apart from the other candidates. When embarking on a contract away from home, you'll need to find somewhere to live, but don't make a long-term commitment to accommodation until your feet are firmly under the table.

Setting Up Your Business

This is where the fun stops, because you'll need to make the right choice between operating via a PAYE Umbrella Company, as a Sole Trader, or as a director of your own Limited Company. In the latter (preferred) case you'll need to register with the HMRC for corporation tax, PAYE, and VAT. You'll need some good accounting software and / or a good accountant, and of course you'll need a company bank account.

Working On Site

When working on site you'll need to make sure that you are adequately insured, that you have strategies for relieving the out-of-office boredom when away from home, and that you submit your timesheets on time. When it comes to office politics, leave the 'permies' to get on with it!

Getting Paid and Paying Tax

You will only get paid for the contract work you undertake if you raise an invoice and if the agency has your correct bank details. If you don't get paid, first try to find out why, and give them another chance before issuing a 'letter before action' to ensure that you do get paid. When operating vai a limited company, pay yourself via a tax-efficient combination of salary, dividends and pension contributions... but beware the dangers of being caught with your pants down by the IR35 and 'income splitting' tax regimes.

--

It's all very well suggesting what you need to do at each stage, but you'll also want to know where to look for the tools and further information that you'll need to help you along the contracting road. You'll need some resources...

Resources

In this book I have given a passing mention to several useful web sites. Here they are again as my collection of useful resources.

The best one-stop-shop for information and advice on all aspects of IT contracting in the UK is the Contractor UK web site at http://www.contractoruk.com/.

When looking for a contract role, you will likely find it on one of the top three UK job sites for IT Contractors, which are:

JobServe at www.jobserve.com

CW Jobs at www.cwjobs.co.uk

Technojobs at www.technojobs.co.uk

(Remember that the Contractor UK job search pulls in jobs from all three of these job sites)

You can get yourself 'well connected' by forming networks of like-minded individuals on Facebook at www.facebook.com or (even better for IT contractors and other professionals) on LinkedIn at www.linkedin.com.

The freelancing web sites at www.elance.com and www.freelancer.com are good for finding additional freelance projects to supplement your contracting income or to tide you over between jobs.

When looking for company accounting software, you will find the market leader in the UK to be Sage, and as an alternative to their PC software package(s) you might consider their SageOne online accounting solution described at:

http://www.sageone.com/

When wrestling with company tax, VAT, and payroll issues your first port of call should be the HMRC web site at www.hmrc.gov.uk, and to run your small PAYE payroll you might find it sufficient to use the HMRC Basic PAYE Tools software available from the Business Link web site at http://www.businesslink.gov.uk/bdotg/action/layer?topicId=10 86857322.

One of the best ways of keeping your skills up-to-date (so that you're always in demand) is by checking out the Computer Based Training (CBT) offerings at http://www.cbtnuggets.com/.

Final Words

I wish you every success in your IT contracting career, but the final words are not from me. They come from one of my favourite quotes:

"Go forward boldly, and unseen forces will come to your aid"

– Earl Nightingale